D1177890

CREATIVE ORIGAMI

by Toyoaki Kawai

translated by
John Clark

HOIKUSHA
保育社

Contents

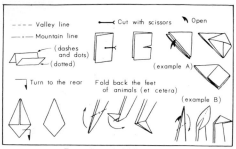

Examples of folding method

CREATIVE ORIGAMI

by Toyoaki Kawai

translated by John Clark

© All rights reserved. No. 35 of Hoikusha's Color Books Series. Published by Hoikusha Pulishing Co., Ltd., 8-6, 4-chome, Tsurumi, Tsurumi-ku, Osaka, 538 Japan. ISBN 4-586-54035-4. First Edition in 1977. 15th Edition in 1989. Printed in JAPAN

FROM TRADITION

TO CREATION

The 'Crane' is the most liked masterpiece of traditional Origami, and is something you might want to try folding in Japanese paper, which will bring out its simple beauty. The 'Flapping Crane' and 'Flapping Crow' have only transformed the traditional 'Crane' a little, and if you take it in your hand and pull the tail as in the photograph, the wings move and children will be delighted.

Crane (traditional) folding method page 4

Flapping crane (creative)
folding method page 5

Flapping crow (creative) folding method page 98

3

Crane (traditional)

①

② Open out in direction of arrow.

③

Fold open the rear side in the same way.

⑤

④

Fold the rear side in the same way.

⑥

Fold open the rear side in the same way.

⑦

⑧

⑨

Fold up in direction of arrow.

⑩

⑪

⑫

Pull out the wings to left and right and swell out the back.

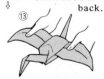
⑬

⑭

Completion

4

Flapping crane (creative)

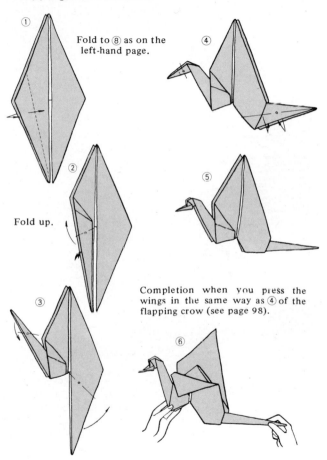

① Fold to ⑧ as on the left-hand page.

② Fold up.

③

④

⑤

Completion when you press the wings in the same way as ④ of the flapping crow (see page 98).

⑥

5

Footman (traditional) folding method page 8

'Footman' is also a very popular traditional origami figure and many forms may be created from its base. 'Small box' and 'Decorative paper ball' are only a few examples.

Small box (creative)
folding method page 98

Decorative paper ball (creative)
folding method page 9

Footman

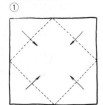

①

⑤

Completion of
Footman

④

Completion of
pleated skirt

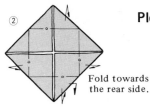

②

Fold towards
the rear side.

Pleated skirt

①

Fold from ④
of 'footman'.

⑤

Completion with
footman's faces
painted in and
pleated skirt
attached.

③

Repeat folding as in ②.

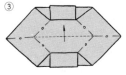

②

Loosen towards
the arrow.

④

Open in direction
of arrow.

③

Take in along the fold-line.

8

Decorative paper ball

①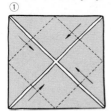

Continue from ② of the left-hand page.

④-A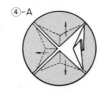

⑧

Fold six pieces of the same form.

②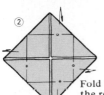

Fold towards the rear side.

⑤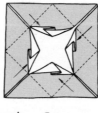

⑨

Glue together the triangular part on the incline.

③

Put in only a fold-line and open out to ①.

⑥

Take in as in ②, ③ and put in a fold-line.

④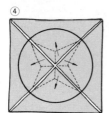

Fold along the fold-line.

⑦

Insert a finger and open out.

⑩

Complete in the same way glueing together the triangular parts.

The traditional 'Offering box' is a simple form which, if you work on the folding method a little, you change into the 'Cat-shaped box' as on the right.

Origami that can amuse as a box will survive real use well when you employ rather thick paper or Japanese paper with a backing. The 'Flower vase' is an adaptation of the basic 'Footman' and 'Crane' which may be enlivened if you put a small vessel with a flower in the middle.

Offering box (traditional) folding method page 12

Cat-shaped box (creative)
folding method page 13

Flower vase (creative)
no explanation of
folding method

11

Offering box

①

②

Fold towards
rear side.

③

④

Open out by the same
method as in ③, ④
and ⑤ on page 4.

⑤

Fold in direction
of arrow.

⑥

⑦

Return to rear.

⑧

Reunite.

⑨

⑩

Do the same for
the rear side.

⑪

⑫

Fold towards
rear side.

⑬

Open out.

⑭

Completion

12

Cat-shaped box

①

Fold to ⑧ on page 12.

②

Also fold the rear side
in the same way.

③

Reunite.

④

⑤

Also fold the rear side
in the same way.

⑥

⑥-A

⑥-B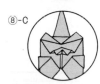

⑦

Return to the rear.

⑧

⑧-A

⑧-B

⑧-C

Make the face in A – C.

⑨
Completion

13

Buffalo (creative) folding method page 100

Bantam hen (creative) folding method page 16

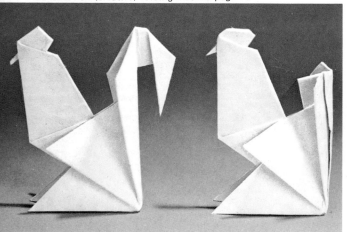

14

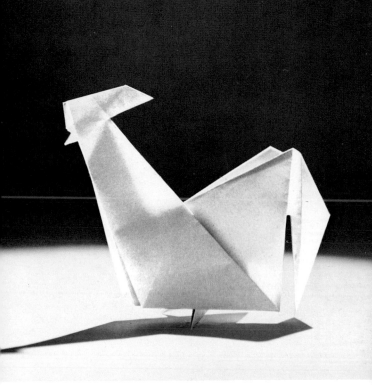

Bantam hen (traditional) folding method page 17

In traditional origami the 'Bantam hen' is a fairly three-dimensional form. The creative origami 'Bantam hen' brings out the feeling of the wings by fold-lines and, in slightly changing the way of folding head and tail, makes cock and hen. The 'Buffalo' is a form made on the base of the traditional 'Bantam hen'.

15

Bantam hen (creative)

①

②

③

Fold to
the rear side.

④

Fold up in direction
of arrow.

⑤

⑥

⑦

⑧

Fold down.

⑨

⑨-A

Make the
cockscomb.

⑩

Completion of cock

⑪

For the hen, fold as
far as ⑧ in the same
way, and fold the tail
down.

⑫

16

Bantam hen (traditional)

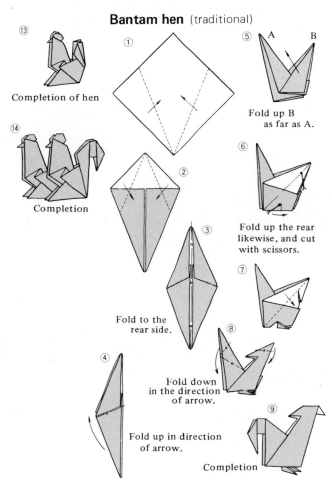

⑬ Completion of hen

⑭ Completion

①

②

③ Fold to the rear side.

④ Fold up in direction of arrow.

⑤ A B
Fold up B as far as A.

⑥ Fold up the rear likewise, and cut with scissors.

⑦

⑧ Fold down in the direction of arrow.

Fold up in direction of arrow.

⑨ Completion

17

The traditional 'Raccoon Dog' is expressed with a slit inserted in the ear section. In the creative 'Raccoon Dog' we have inserted no slit and tried to create a much more three-dimensional figure.

Raccoon (creative) folding method page 20

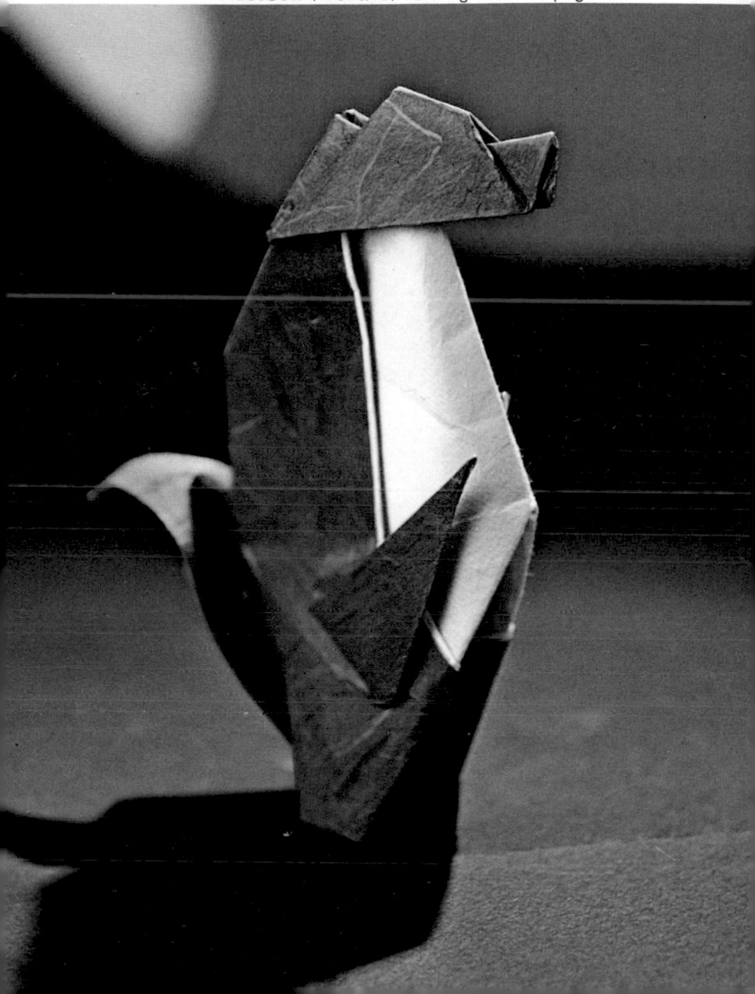

Raccoon (creative)

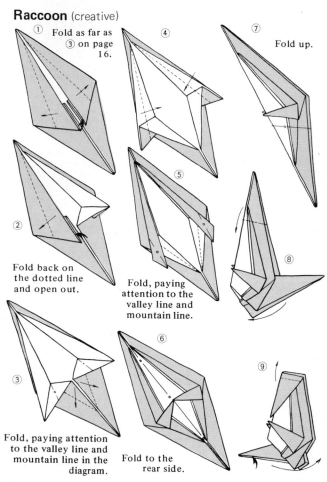

① Fold as far as ③ on page 16.

② Fold back on the dotted line and open out.

③ Fold, paying attention to the valley line and mountain line in the diagram.

④

⑤ Fold, paying attention to the valley line and mountain line.

⑥ Fold to the rear side.

⑦ Fold up.

⑧

⑨

20

Raccoon (traditional)

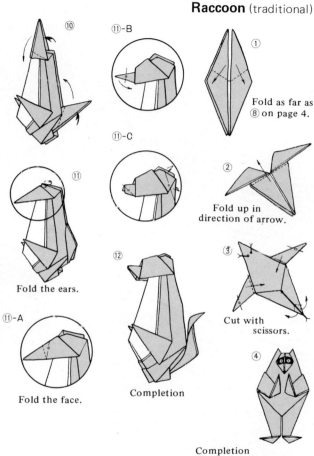

⑩

⑪-B

⑪-C

⑪

Fold the ears.

⑫

⑪-A

Fold the face.

Completion

①

Fold as far as ⑧ on page 4.

②

Fold up in direction of arrow.

③

Cut with scissors.

④

Completion when you paint the face.

21

This is a Japanese 'Ghost' which can be simply made from the base of the 'Crane'. We have also made the face in the creative form. You can also go as far as to make the splendid mask on the right-hand page on the base of the 'Crane'.

African Mask (creative)
no explanation of folding method

Ghost (creative)
folding method page 25

23

Ghost (traditional)

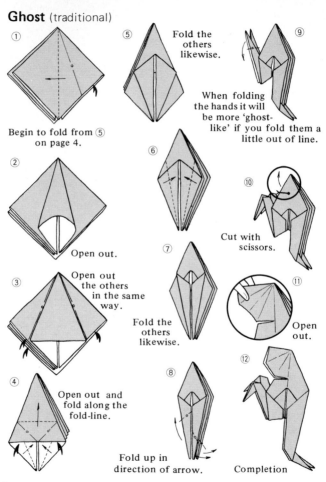

① Begin to fold from ⑤ on page 4.

② Open out.

③ Open out the others in the same way.

④ Open out and fold along the fold-line.

⑤ Fold the others likewise.

⑥

⑦ Fold the others likewise.

⑧ Fold up in direction of arrow.

⑨ When folding the hands it will be more 'ghost-like' if you fold them a little out of line.

⑩ Cut with scissors.

⑪ Open out.

⑫ Completion

24

Ghost (creative)

①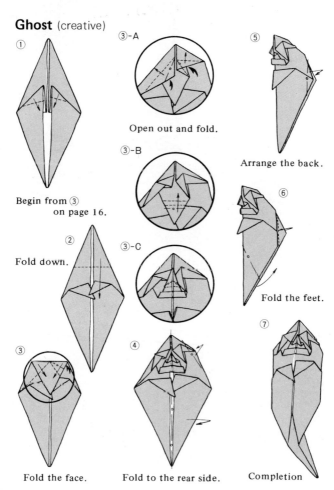

Begin from ③
on page 16.

② Fold down.

③ Fold the face.

③-A Open out and fold.

③-B

③-C

④ Fold to the rear side.

⑤ Arrange the back.

⑥ Fold the feet.

⑦ Completion

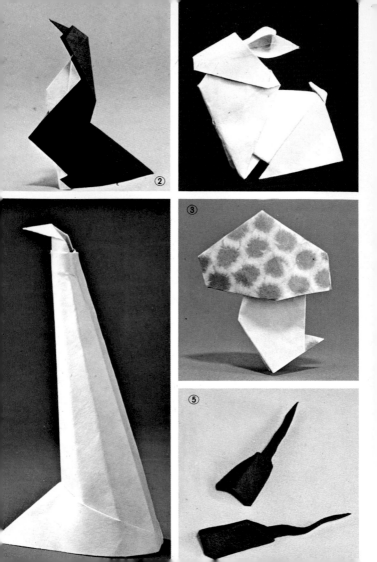

The traditional 'Rabbit' is flat and simplified, and only the long ears may be considered rabbit-like. The creative form expresses the rabbit's plump loveableness, and shows a little movement. Other works can be folded from the same base.

Rabbit (traditional) folding method page 29

Mushroom

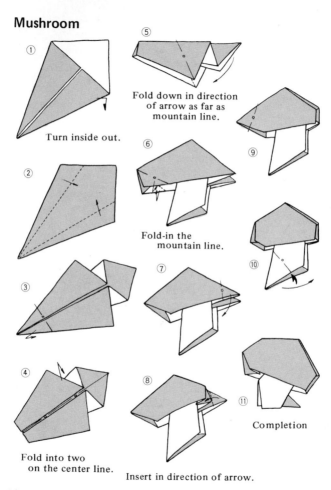

① Turn inside out.

②

③

④ Fold into two on the center line.

⑤ Fold down in direction of arrow as far as mountain line.

⑥ Fold-in the mountain line.

⑦

⑧ Insert in direction of arrow.

⑨

⑩

⑪ Completion

Rabbit (traditional)

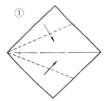

①

⑤

Fold down.

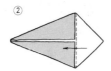

②

⑥

③

⑦

Fold up likewise.

④

Cut with scissors.

⑧

Completion when you paint the face.

29

In Japan there is a custom on formal occasions to affix a handmade gift decoration to a present. The creative form is that of the 'Crane-shaped gift envelope' and 'Purse'. The 'Crane-shaped gift envelope' is lined by red and white.

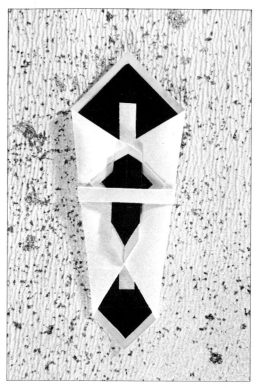

Gift decoration (traditional) folding method page 32

folding method page 105

(creative) folding method page 32

Gift decoration

①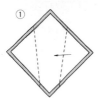

Place two paper pieces of different sizes on top of each other.

②

Fold as in the dotted line.

③

④

Pay attention to the mountain line and valley line.

⑤

Cut the paper to put in as belt and padding.

⑥

⑦ Completion

Crane-shaped gift envelope

①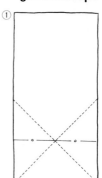

Put in fold-lines only on a paper rectangle, and open out.

②

Press in direction of arrow, and take in along the fold-line.

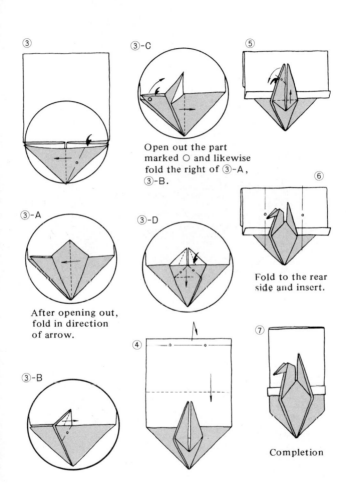

③

③-C

Open out the part
marked ○ and likewise
fold the right of ③-A,
③-B.

⑤

③-A

After opening out,
fold in direction
of arrow.

③-D

⑥

Fold to the rear
side and insert.

③-B

④

⑦

Completion

Treasure ship (traditional) folding method page 36

The 'Treasure ship' which together with the 'Crane' is known for its excellent form should certainly be folded with backed Japanese paper. You can even float the 'House boat' on water and play with it.

Yacht (creative) folding method page 37

Houseboat (creative)
no explanation of
folding method

35

Treasure ship

①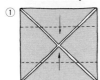

②

Open out.

③

Open out in the same way as ②.

④

Fold towards the rear side.

⑤

Open out in direction of arrow.

⑥

Open out in direction of arrow.

⑦

Loosen the right side in direction of arrow.

⑧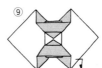

Loosen the left side likewise.

⑨

Return to rear.

⑩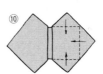

⑪

⑫

Fold in two at the middle.

⑬

⑭

Pull in direction of arrow as in the diagram.

⑮

Completion

36

Yacht

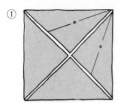

①

Fold the line part to the inside.

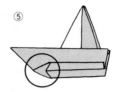

⑤

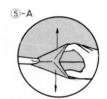

⑤-A

Refer to example B on page 97.

②

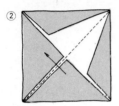

③

Fold up in direction of arrow.

⑥

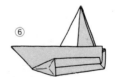

④

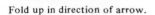

⑦

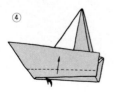

Completion

37

With the traditional 'Fox-mask', you must draw in the eyes and whiskers. The two creative masks are intended for adults and are enjoyed in expressing the individuality of the person folding them. With the 'Water-goblin mask' execute the folding of the mouth part carefully.

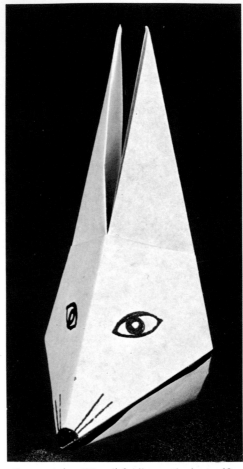

Fox-mask (traditional) folding method page 40

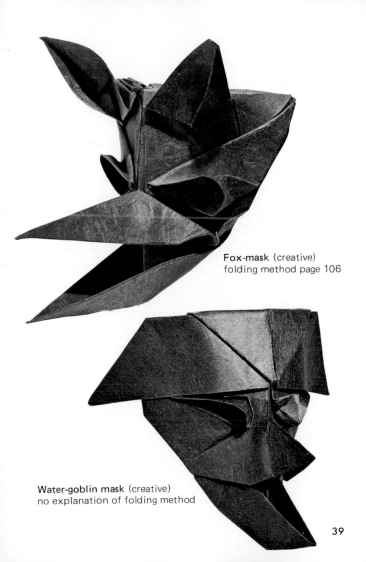

Fox-mask (creative)
folding method page 106

Water-goblin mask (creative)
no explanation of folding method

Fox-mask (traditional)

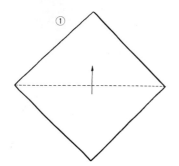

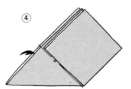

Open out the rear side
likewise.

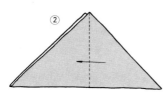

Open out in direction of arrow.

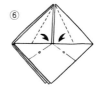

Open out and fold.

⑦

⑩

Paint the eyes and
nose to complete.

⑧

Return to rear.

⑨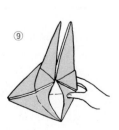

The 'Jet plane' can be made from newspaper. See how well it flies!

Jet plane (traditional) folding method page 44

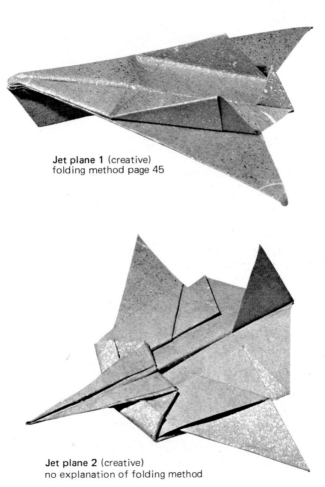

Jet plane 1 (creative)
folding method page 45

Jet plane 2 (creative)
no explanation of folding method

43

Jet plane (traditional)

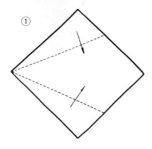

①

②

③

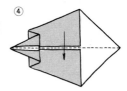

④

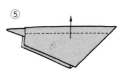

⑤

Fold up in direction
of arrow.

⑥

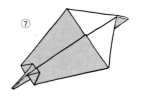

⑦

Completion

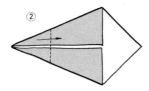

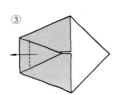

Jet plane 1 (creative)

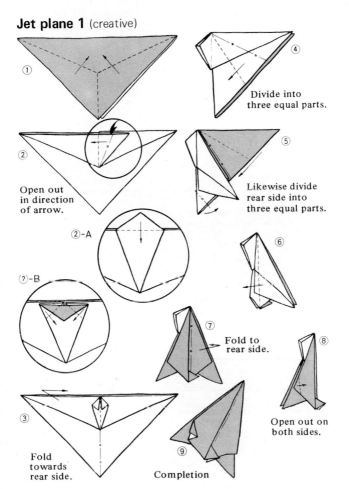

①

② Open out in direction of arrow.

②-A

②-B

③ Fold towards rear side.

④ Divide into three equal parts.

⑤ Likewise divide rear side into three equal parts.

⑥

⑦ Fold to rear side.

⑧ Open out on both sides.

⑨ Completion

45

With the traditional 'Frog' pay attention to the folding of the legs. The creative 'Tree frog' will hop when you press down the behind. With the 'Three monkeys' you can make the three poses of 'See no evil, speak no evil, hear no evil' by the folding of the hands.

Frog (traditional)
folding method page 48

Tree frog (creative)
folding method page 49

Frog (traditional)

① Fold as far as ⑤ on page 4.

② Open out.

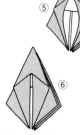

⑤

⑥ Likewise fold the other parts.

③ Likewise open out the other parts.

⑦

⑧

⑨ Fold up in direction of arrow.

⑩

⑪ Fold hands and feet.

⑫ Completion

48

Tree frog (creative)

①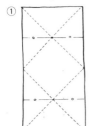

Fold with a rectangle.

②

Tuck in
on fold-lines
and return to rear.

③

③-A

Refer to
example A on Page 97.

④

Return to rear.

⑤

⑥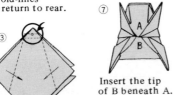

⑦

A
B

Insert the tip
of B beneath A.

⑧

⑧-A

⑧-B

⑨

Cut with scissors.

⑨-A

Set both tips upright
and make the eyes.

⑩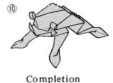

Completion

49

If you compare the two 'Cicadas' you will easily see the differences between traditional and creative origami.

You can make the 'Owl' from the same base as the creative 'Cicada'.

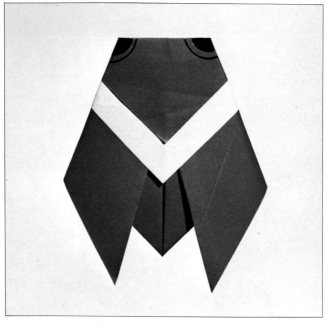

Cicada (traditional) folding method page 52

Cicada (creative) folding method page 53

Owl (creative) folding method page 110

Cicada (traditional)

①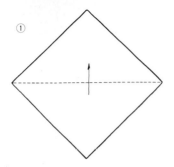

②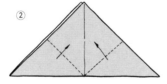

③

④

⑤

Fold the dotted line
part towards you.

⑥

Fold towards the
rear side.

⑦

Draw in the eyes.

⑧

Completion

Cicada (creative)

①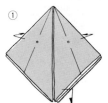

Fold from ③ on the
left-hand page.

②

③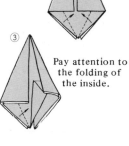

Pay attention to
the folding of
the inside.

④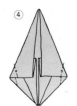

⑤

⑥

⑦

Return to rear.

⑧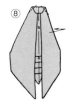

⑨

Bend the torso
section a little
in direction of
arrow.

⑩

Completion

Display box (traditional) folding method page 56

Box with mask (creative) no explanation of folding method

This has a mask folded out from the four triangles of the traditional 'Display box'. The first step to creative origami is in work which adds something to the simple form. In the 'Box with lid' take care with the side of the box and lid.

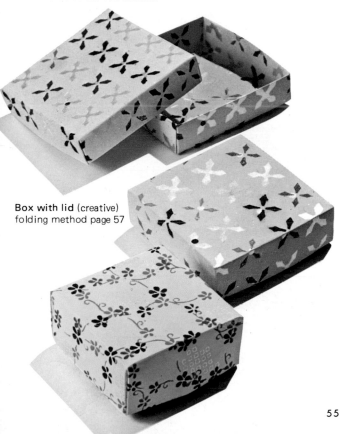

Box with lid (creative)
folding method page 57

Display box

①

Fold as far as ⑤ on page 4, and open out in direction of arrow.

②

Fold towards rear side.

③

Fold the rear in the same way as ① and ②.

④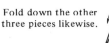

⑤

Fold down the other three pieces likewise.

⑥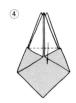

Open out the inside.

⑦

Completion

56

Box with lid

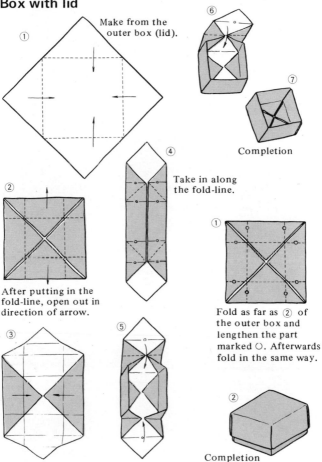

Make from the outer box (lid).

①

② After putting in the fold-line, open out in direction of arrow.

③

④ Take in along the fold-line.

⑤

⑥

⑦ Completion

① Fold as far as ② of the outer box and lengthen the part marked ○. Afterwards fold in the same way.

② Completion

57

Sea bream (traditional) folding method page 60

Helmet (traditional) folding method page 60

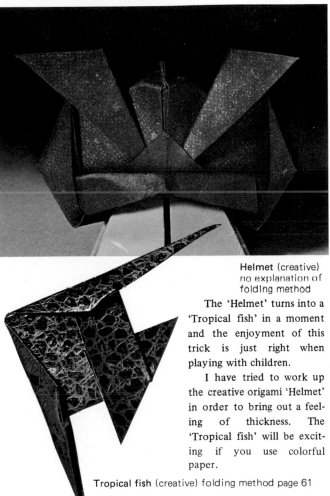

Helmet (creative)
no explanation of
folding method

The 'Helmet' turns into a
'Tropical fish' in a moment
and the enjoyment of this
trick is just right when
playing with children.

I have tried to work up
the creative origami 'Helmet'
in order to bring out a feeling of thickness. The
'Tropical fish' will be excit-
ing if you use colorful
paper.

Tropical fish (creative) folding method page 61

Helmet, Sea bream (traditional)

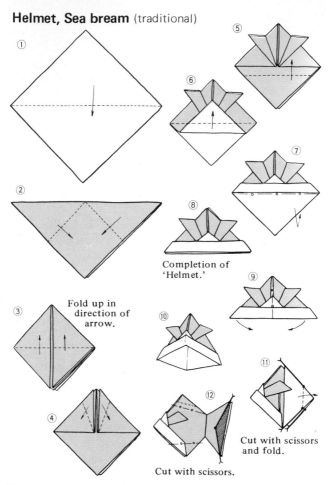

①

⑤

⑥

②

⑦

③ Fold up in direction of arrow.

⑧ Completion of 'Helmet.'

⑨

⑩

④

⑪ Cut with scissors and fold.

⑫ Cut with scissors.

Tropical fish

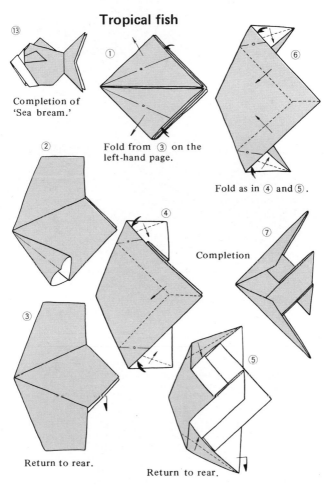

⑬ Completion of 'Sea bream.'

① Fold from ③ on the left-hand page.

②

③ Return to rear.

④

⑤ Return to rear.

⑥ Fold as in ④ and ⑤.

⑦ Completion

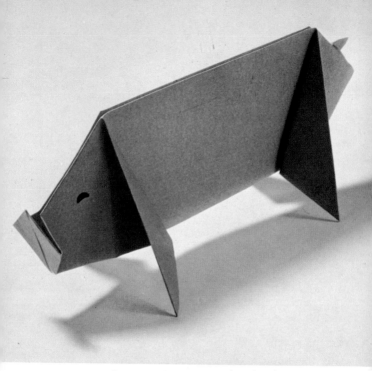

Pig (traditional) folding method page 64

The 'Pig' can be made simply even by children, but the folding of the nose section can be tricky. You fold it from a very simple base which can also make the room decoration 'Ornament' and the attractive 'Cat'. Four 'Ornaments' folded one after another can be stuck together, so why not think of a pleasant color scheme?

Ornament (creative) folding method page 65

Cat (creative) folding method page 112

Pig

①

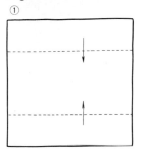

④

Fold in two at the middle.

②

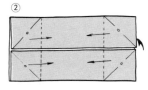

③

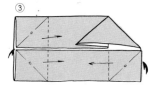

Fold the others likewise.

⑤

⑥

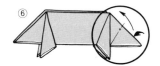

⑥-A

Fold the tail.

Ornament

⑥-B

⑥-C

①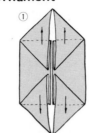

Fold as far as ④ on the left-hand page.

②

Insert B into A.

③

④

Fold the same into four.

⑤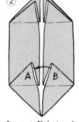

Apply glue to the slant line part and stick down.

⑥

Completion

⑦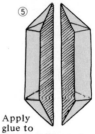

⑧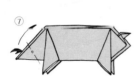

Completion

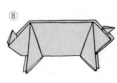

65

Parakeet (creative) folding method page 114

66   **Small pigeon** (creative) folding method page 68

It is all right not to paint in the eyes and wings on the traditional 'Parakeet'.

Parakeet (traditional) folding method page 69

Small pigeon

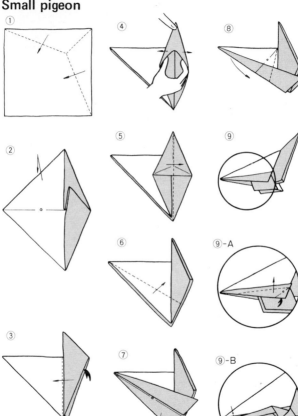

① ④ ⑧

② ⑤ ⑨

③ ⑨-A

Refer to example B
on page 97.

⑥

⑦

Fold up in the
same way.

⑨-B

68

Parakeet (traditional)

⑩

⑪

⑫

Completion

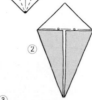
①

②

③

Open out in direction
of arrow.

④

⑤

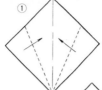
⑥

⑦

Cut with scissors
and fold.

⑧

Completion of
'Parakeet'

①

Fold as far as ⑥ of
'Parakeet' (do not
insert scissors in
the tail section).

②

You can finish it into
'lovebird'.

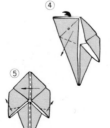

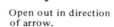

69

Carp pennant (traditional) folding method page 72

Sitting-up Dog (creative)
folding method page 72

In Japan it is the custom to raise a Carp pennant on the fifth of May. The 'Goat' and 'Dog' are made from the same base as the 'Carp pennant'.

Goat (creative) folding method page 116

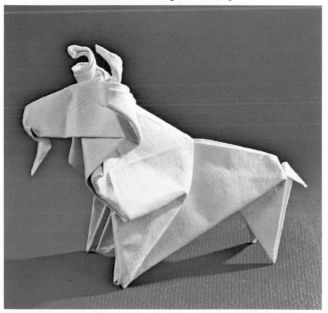

Carp pennant

Sitting-up Dog

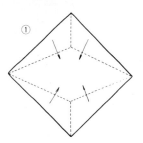

①

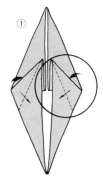

①

Fold from ② of the 'Carp pennant'.

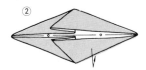

②

① -A

Refer to example B on page 97.

③

Cut with scissors.

① -B

④

Completion

72

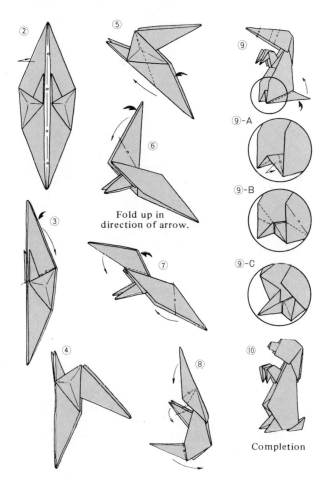

② ③ ④ ⑤

⑥ Fold up in direction of arrow.

⑦ ⑧

⑨ ⑨-A ⑨-B ⑨-C

⑩ Completion

Magic boat (traditional) folding method page 76

(Sailing boat)

(Catamaran)

First make a 'Catamaran' and with one fold turn it into a 'Sailing boat'. From this base I was able to make the completely different 'Vase' and 'Sled'.

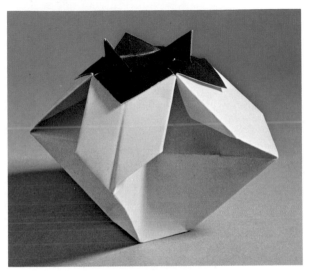

Vase (creative) folding method page 77

Sled (creative) no explanation of folding method

Magic boat

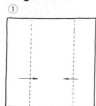
(1)

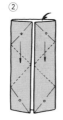
(2)

Open out in
direction of arrow.

(3)

Open out likewise.

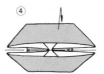
(4)

Fold into two
in the middle.

(5)

Completion of
Catamaran

From 'Catamaran'
to 'Sailing boat'

(1)

Pull in direction of arrow.

(2)

(3)

(4)

Completion of
'Sailing boat'.

Vase

①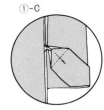

Fold as far as ④ on the left-hand page.

①-C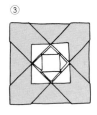

③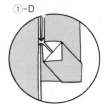

①-A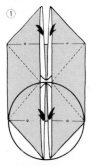

①-D

④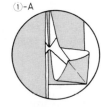

Open out the middle.

①-B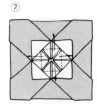

②

Fold the other three corners in the same way.

⑤

Completion

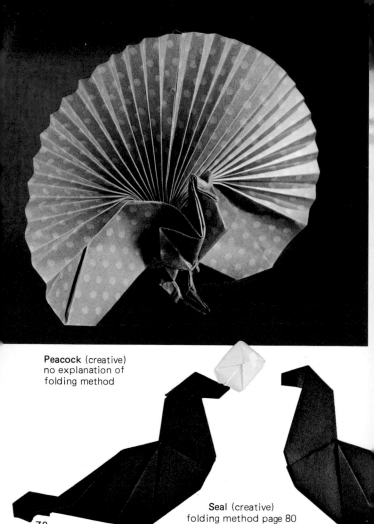

Peacock (creative)
no explanation of
folding method

Seal (creative)
folding method page 80

78

Seal (traditional) folding method page 81

These are the traditional and creative origami 'Seal'. The creative one is considered much closer to the form of the real one. You fold the 'Peacock' from a paper rectangle folding the torso with half (from the base of 'Crane') and with the remaining half you fold the wings in a concertina. This is also an example of adaptation with a simple base.

Seal (creative)

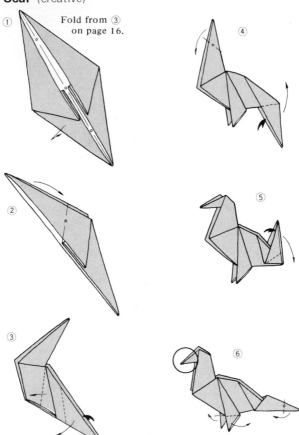

① Fold from ③ on page 16.

②

③

④

⑤

⑥

80

Seal (traditional)

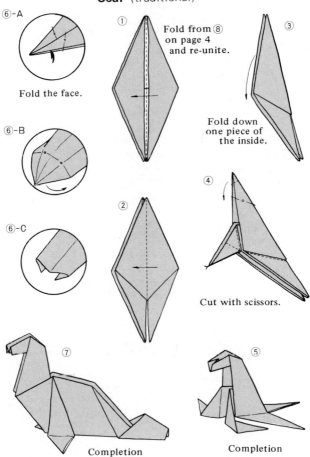

⑥-A
Fold the face.

⑥-B

⑥-C

① Fold from ⑧ on page 4 and re-unite.

②

③ Fold down one piece of the inside.

④ Cut with scissors.

⑤ Completion

⑦ Completion

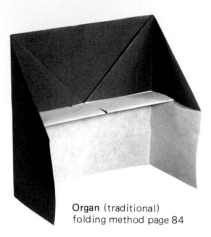

The folding of the 'Organ' and the 'Paper fold' is simple and you can use Japanese paper if you back it with figured paper. The 'Paper fold' is quite suitable as a cardholder too.

Organ (traditional)
folding method page 84

Paper fold (creative) folding method page 118

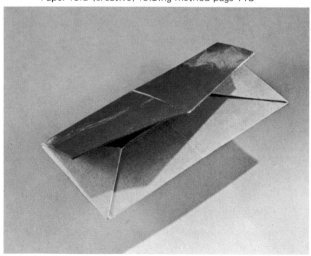

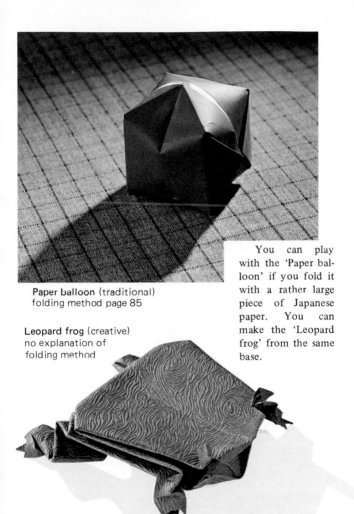

Paper balloon (traditional)
folding method page 85

Leopard frog (creative)
no explanation of
folding method

You can play with the 'Paper balloon' if you fold it with a rather large piece of Japanese paper. You can make the 'Leopard frog' from the same base.

83

Organ

①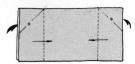

Open out in direction of arrow.

②

③

④

⑤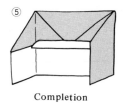

Completion

84

Paper balloon

①

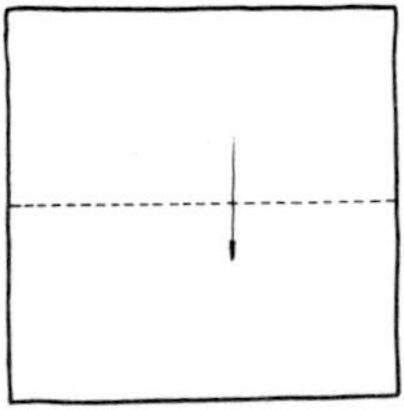

②

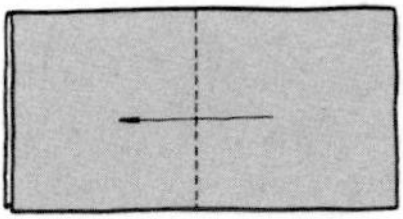

③ 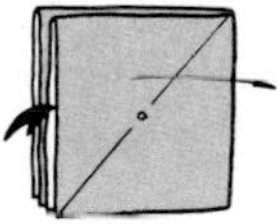 Open out.

④ Open out the rear side likewise.

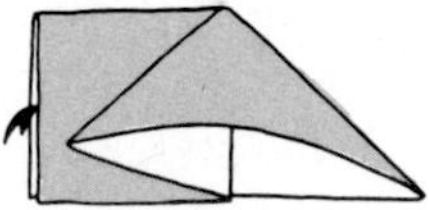

⑤

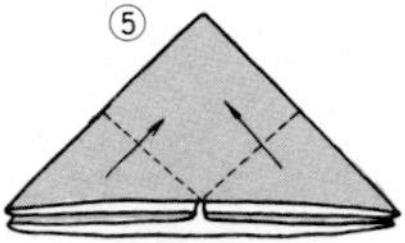

⑥

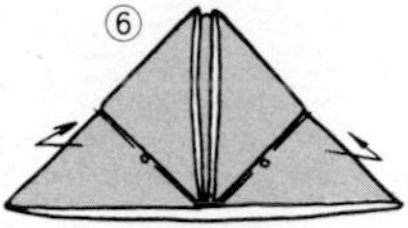

⑦

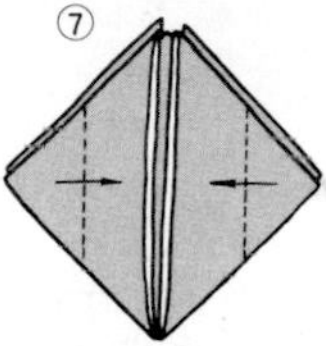

⑧

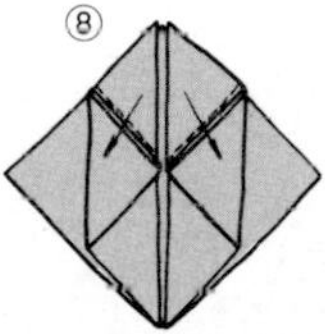

⑨

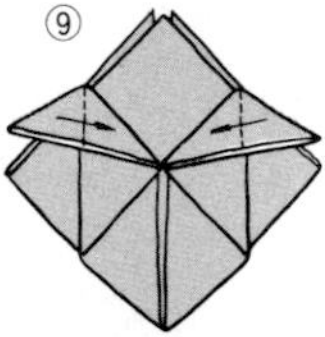

⑩

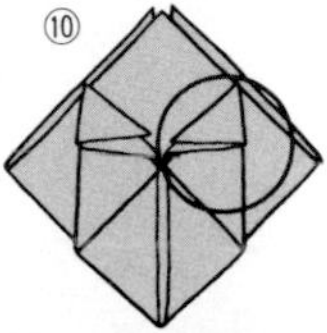

⑩-A 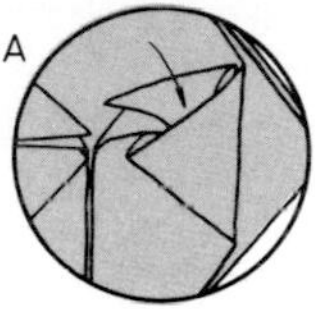 Insert.

⑪ Fold the rear side likewise.

Blow in air.

⑫ Completion

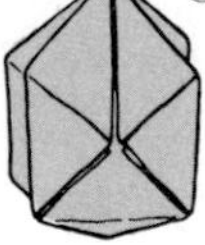

85

Eagle (traditional) folding method page 88

Both forms of the 'Eagle' are produced from the base of the 'Crane'. The creative one seems to express much more the strength of the predators. The important features to work on are the folding of beak, feet, etc. Try folding them with a rather thick Western paper or a backed Japanese paper.

Eagle (creative) folding method page 119 ⇨

Eagle (traditional)

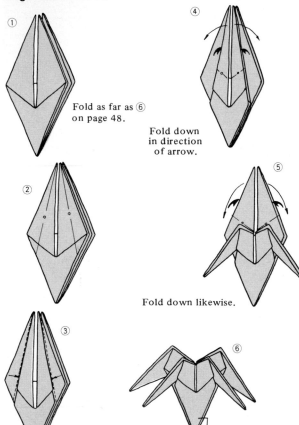

① Fold as far as ⑥ on page 48.

④ Fold down in direction of arrow.

②

⑤ Fold down likewise.

③

⑥ Return to rear.

88

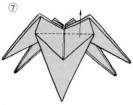

⑦

Fold the line part upwards.

⑩

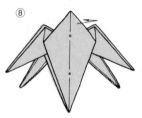

⑧

Fold into two at the middle.

⑪

Completion

⑨

Mandarin duck (traditional) folding method page 92

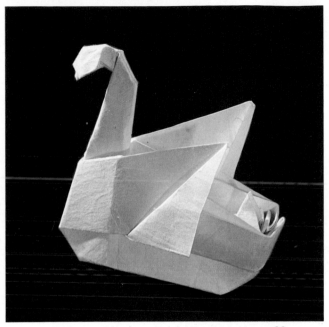

Swan container (creative) folding method page 92

The shape of the duck is simple and a suitable source material for origami. With the traditional 'Mandarin duck' you insert a slit and fold. For the creative origami figure we have devised an elegant 'Swan container'. With the folding of the head section please look at a real swan and study it carefully.

Mandarin duck

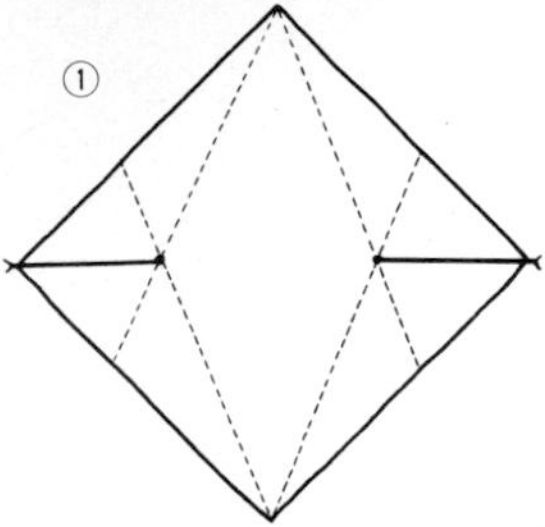

Swan container

①

Put in a crease and
cut with scissors.

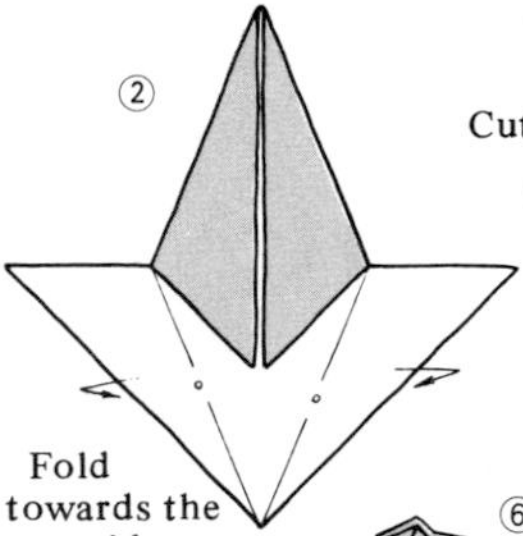

②

Fold
towards the
rear side.

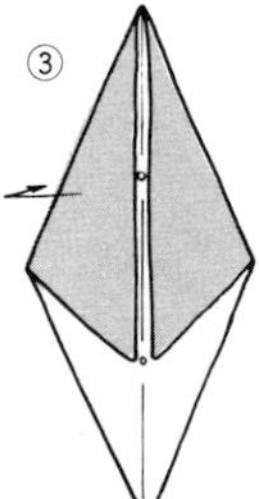

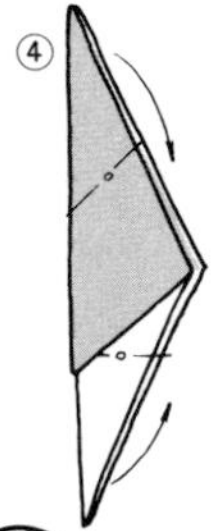

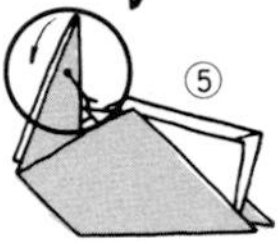

③

④

⑤

Cut with scissors.

⑤-A

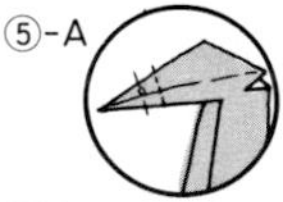

This is the head
of a male.
Cut slit.

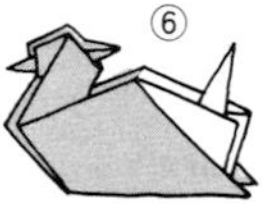

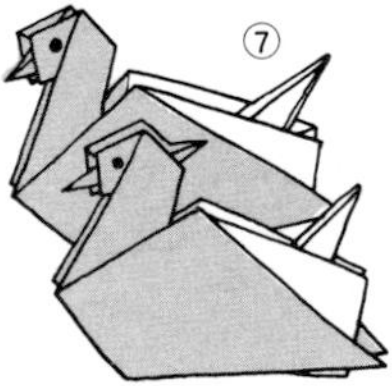

⑥

⑦

Completion

①

②

③

④

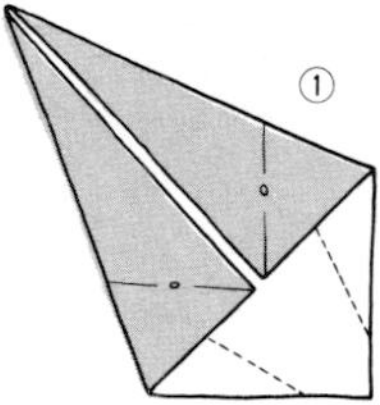

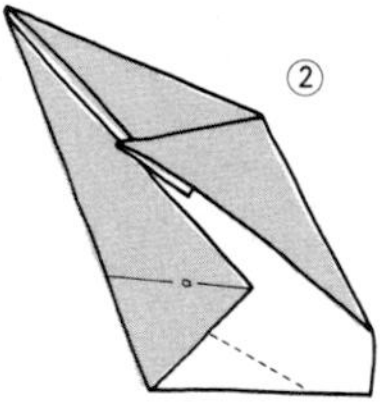

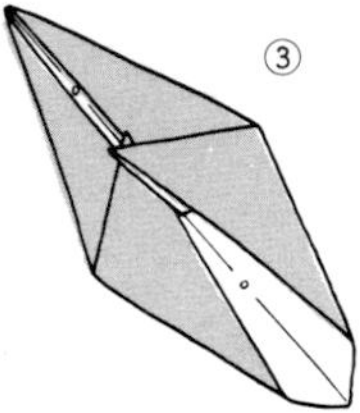

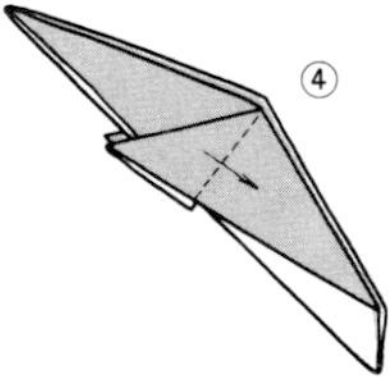

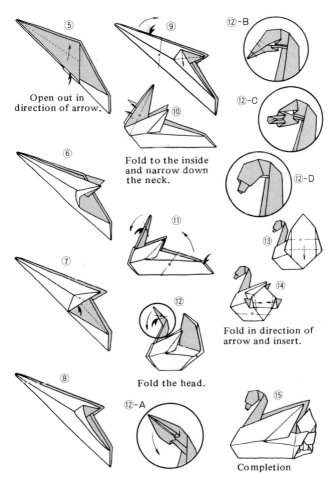

⑤ Open out in direction of arrow.

⑥

⑦

⑧

⑨

⑩ Fold to the inside and narrow down the neck.

⑪

⑫ Fold the head.

⑫-A

⑫-B

⑫-C

⑫-D

⑬

⑭ Fold in direction of arrow and insert.

⑮ Completion

The traditional 'Farm house' is from the same base as the 'Catamaran.' Since it was a little too simple I have tried to make a three-dimensional house. It will be sturdy if folded with thick Western paper and if you lift the roof you can use the inside as a container. The 'Snow child' is made from the same base as the creative 'Farm house'.

Snow child (creative) ⇨ no explanation of folding method

Farm house (traditional) folding method page 96

Farm house (creative) folding method page 120

Farm house (traditional)

①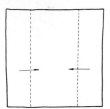

②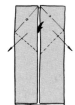

Open out.

③

④

Completion

96

Essentials of folding the parts

Example A

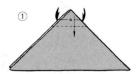

①

②

Insert a finger.

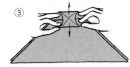

③

Open out in direction of arrow.

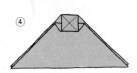

④

Example B

①

②

Open out in direction of arrow with thumb and forefinger.

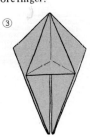

③

Flapping crow (creative)

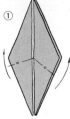

①

Fold as far as ① on page 4. Fold as in the arrow.

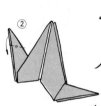

②

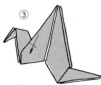

③

Fold the wings only at the dotted line section.

④

Press down softly with your finger.

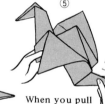

⑤

When you pull the tail in direction of arrow, the wings move. Completion

Small box (creative)

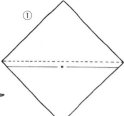

①

Made from the outer box (lid).

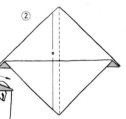

②

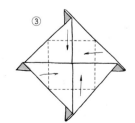

③

④

Open out in direction of arrow.

⑤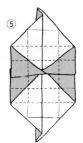

Take up along the fold-line.

⑥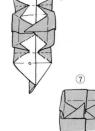

⑦

⑧

Turn the box inside down and insert scissors.

⑨

Raise up the fold-line part.

⑨-A

⑨-B

Cut with scissors.

⑨-C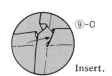

Insert.

⑩

Completion

①

Fold as far as ④ of the outer box, put in a fold line so that it will be smaller than the outer box.

②

Fold in the same way as ⑤, ⑥, and ⑦ of the outer box.

③

Completion

Buffalo (creative)

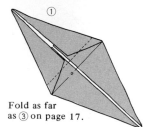

① Fold as far as ③ on page 17.

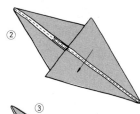

②

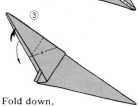

③ Fold down.

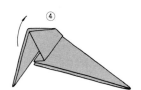

④

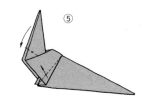

⑤

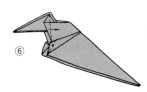

⑥

⑦ Open out the head part.

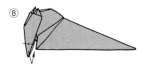

⑧

⑨

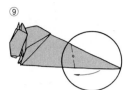

⑩

⑨-A

⑪

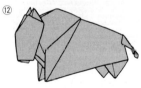

Twist the tip of the tail.

⑨-B

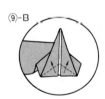

⑫

Completion

⑨-C

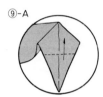

101

Rabbit (creative)

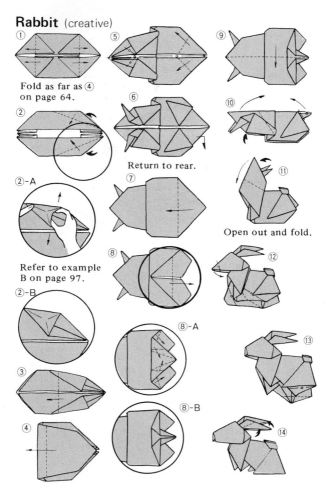

① Fold as far as ④ on page 64.

②

②-A Refer to example B on page 97.

②-B

③

④

⑤

⑥ Return to rear.

⑦

⑧

⑧-A

⑧-B

⑨

⑩

⑪ Open out and fold.

⑫

⑬

⑭

Penguin (creative)

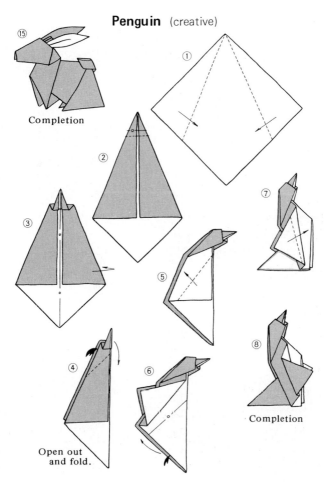

⑮ Completion

①

②

③

④ Open out and fold.

⑤

⑥

⑦

⑧ Completion

Tadpole (creative)

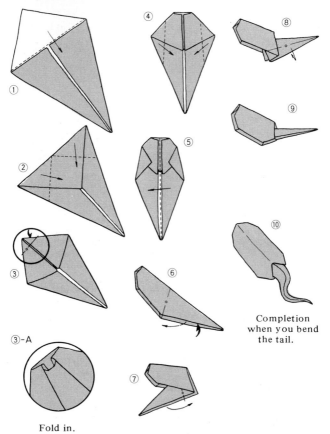

① ② ③

③-A

Fold in.

④ ⑤ ⑥ ⑦

⑧ ⑨ ⑩

Completion
when you bend
the tail.

104

Purse (creative)

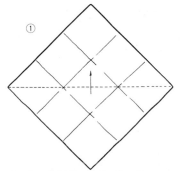

① Put in a fold-line as in the diagram and fold in two.

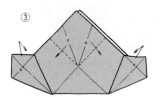

② Open out.

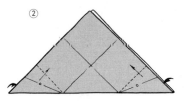

③

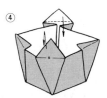

④

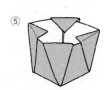

⑤

⑥ Fold so as to twist it.

⑦ Completion

Fox-mask (creative)

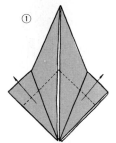

①

Fold from ⑦ on page 4.

③

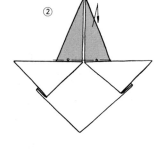

②

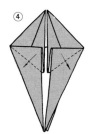

④

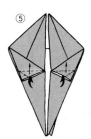

⑤

Make the eyes.

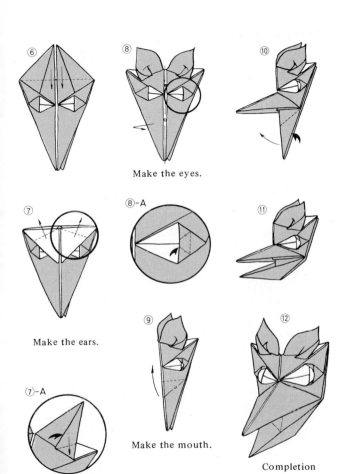

⑥

⑧
Make the eyes.

⑩

⑦
Make the ears.

⑧-A

⑪

⑦-A

⑨
Make the mouth.

⑫
Completion

Fold the other ear likewise.

107

Three monkeys (creative)

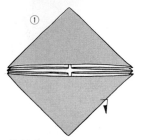

①

Fold from ② on page 49.

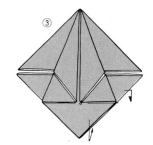

③

Return to rear.

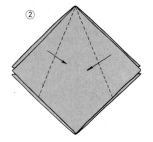

②

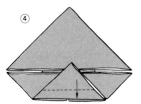

④

⑤

⑥

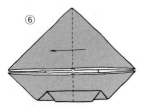

⑧-A

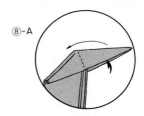

⑧-B

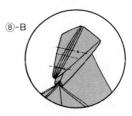

⑦

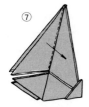

⑨

Expression of the
hand will change
with location of
the fold-line.

⑧

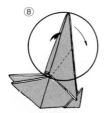

Open out the head section.

⑩

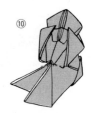

Completion

109

Owl (creative)

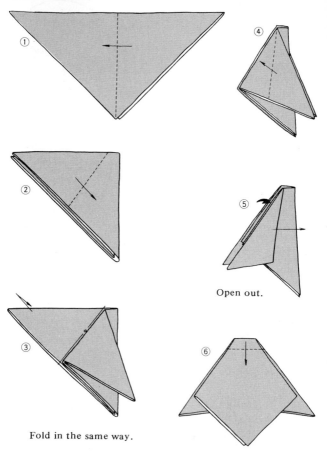

①

②

③ Fold in the same way.

④

⑤ Open out.

⑥

110

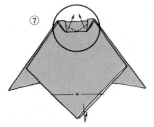

Fold the head section.

Fold the feet.

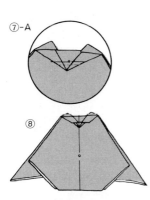

Completion

Cat (creative)

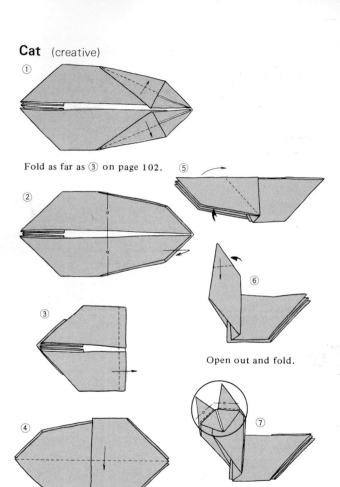

①

Fold as far as ③ on page 102.

②

③

④

⑤

⑥

Open out and fold.

⑦

Fold so the face is towards the front.

112

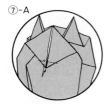

⑦-A

⑨

The rear legs and tail are the same as ⑥, ⑦, ⑧, ⑨ and ⑩ on page 102.

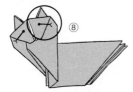

⑧

Insert scissors.

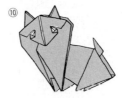

⑩

Completion when you do the folding of legs as in ⑫ and ⑬ on page 103.

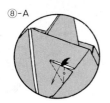

⑧-A

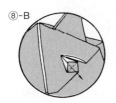

⑧-B

113

Parakeet (creative)

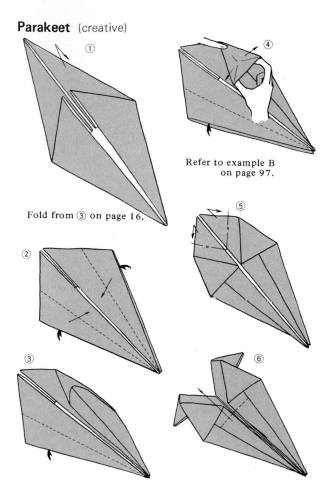

① Fold from ③ on page 16.

②

③

④ Refer to example B on page 97.

⑤

⑥

114

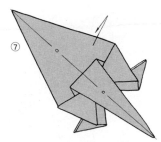

⑦

Fold towards the rear side.

⑧-B

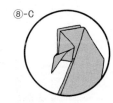

⑧-C

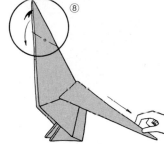

⑧

Pull the tail in direction of arrow.

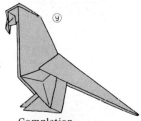

⑨

Completion

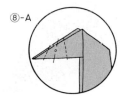

⑧-A

Goat (creative)

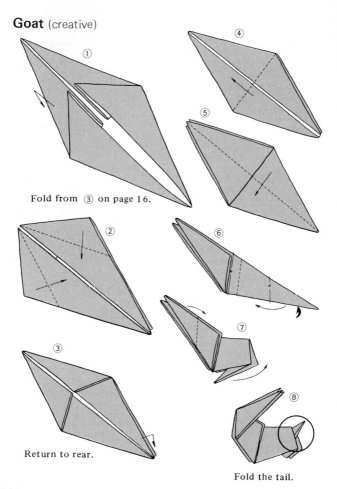

① Fold from ③ on page 16.

②

③ Return to rear.

④

⑤

⑥

⑦

⑧ Fold the tail.

116

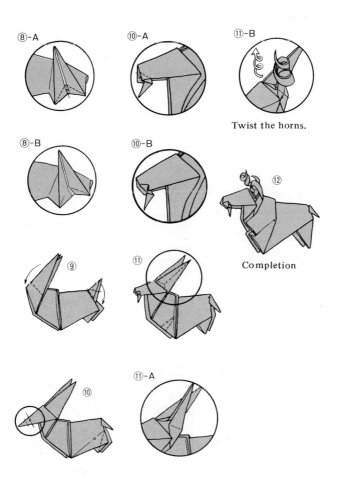

⑧-A

⑩-A

⑪-B

Twist the horns.

⑧-B

⑩-B

⑫

Completion

⑨

⑪

⑩

⑪-A

Paper fold (creative)

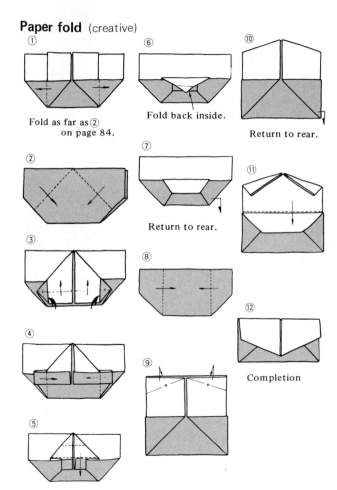

① Fold as far as ② on page 84.

②

③

④

⑤

⑥ Fold back inside.

⑦ Return to rear.

⑧

⑨

⑩ Return to rear.

⑪

⑫ Completion

Eagle (creative)

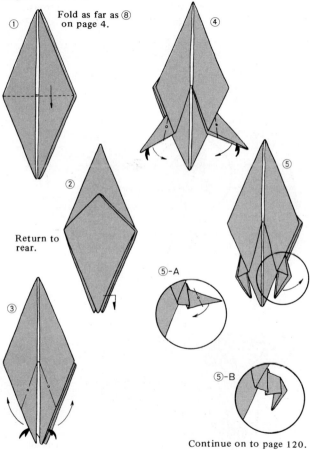

① Fold as far as ⑧ on page 4.

② Return to rear.

③

④

⑤

⑤-A

⑤-B

Continue on to page 120.

119

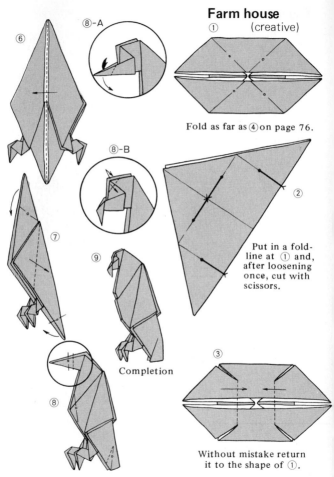

Farm house
(creative)

① Fold as far as ④ on page 76.

② Put in a fold-line at ① and, after loosening once, cut with scissors.

③ Without mistake return it to the shape of ①.

⑥

⑦

⑧

⑧-A

⑧-B

⑨ Completion

120

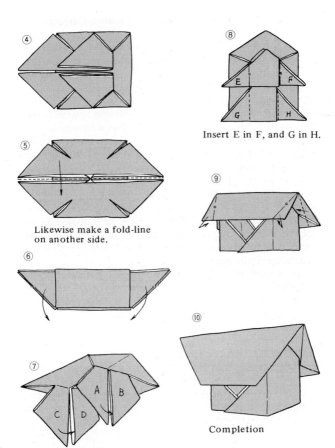

④

⑤

Likewise make a fold-line on another side.

⑥

⑦

Insert A in B, and C in D.

⑧

Insert E in F, and G in H.

⑨

⑩

Completion

121

From Traditional Origami to Creative Origami

It is not known when or by whom traditional origami was originated, only that it is the folded paper craft from Japan's ancient past. After the war, however, creative origami was devised in some people's attempts to make something new. They did not want to be bored by simply imitating a folding method, though there were many places where creative origami learned its basic folds from traditional origami. This is because however complicated and elaborated creative origami was, its basic folding method had several important points in common with traditional origami.

What are the important differences between the two kinds of origami? One is that traditional origami is comparatively planar with great abbreviation. Creative origami is however three-dimentional and carefully copies the outstanding features of the real object. Even the fold-lines comply with the model, wasteful creases are eliminated, and the object's essential features are firmly seized.

The second difference is that if you fold traditional origami according to a diagram it will always be finished the same whoever folded it. But with creative origami the form will always have a different feel according to the person who folded it.

When you fold creative origami it is essential to fully consider the form you will be trying to fold. Please take care especially when the result will not look like that of the real object. Enjoy these differences. This latitude will be a step towards future creation.

If you can do traditional origami, it is not an overstatement to say that eventually you will be able to produce excellent creative origami figures as well.

Backing of Japanese paper

Backing is the gluing together of two sheets of paper. When you back Japanese paper, the paper is firm and easy to fold. Match the colors well when the paper's rear surface will show.

The method is as follows:

(1) Cut two sheets of paper of suitable size.
(2) Put one sheet on a flat surface, dissolve pure starch in water and dilute a little. If the glue is too thick the paper will be stiff, thick, and difficult to fold. Spread the paste with a brush.
(3) First apply the paste widely over the diagonals, and next vertically and laterally. Then spread it evenly over the whole outwards from the center.
(4) Place another sheet of paper on top, and rub over with a dry brush. Use the brush as in (3), spreading from the center outwards to press out the air in the middle without making wrinkles.
(5) Let dry, cut into a square and use.

Finishing of works

When the work is completed glue the tips together. This way, you can preserve and display it permanently.

HOIKUSHA COLOR BOOKS

ENGLISH EDITIONS

Book Size 4″×6″

① KATSURA
② TOKAIDO Hiroshige
③ EMAKI
④ KYOTO
⑤ UKIYOE
⑥ GEM STONES
⑦ NARA
⑧ TOKYO Past and Present
⑨ KYOTO GARDENS
⑩ IKEBANA
⑪ KABUKI
⑫ JAPANESE CASTLES
⑬ JAPANESE
 FESTIVALS
⑭ WOOD-BLOCK
 PRINTING
⑮ N O H
⑯ HAWAII
⑰ JAPAN
⑱ BUDDHIST IMAGES
⑲ OSAKA
⑳ HOKUSAI
㉑ ORIGAMI
㉒ JAPANESE SWORDS
㉓ GOLDFISH
㉔ SUMI-E
㉕ SHELLS OF JAPAN

㉖ FOLK ART
㉗ TOKYO NIKKO FUJI
㉘ NATIONAL FLAGS
㉙ BONSAI
㉚ UTAMARO
㉛ TEA CEREMONY
㉜ PAPER DOLLS
㉝ JAPANESE CERAMICS
㉞ MODEL CARS
㉟ CREATIVE ORIGAMI
㊱ Z E N
㊲ KIMONO
㊳ CHINESE COOKING
㊴ KYOGEN
㊵ NOH MASKS
㊶ LIVING ORIGAMI
㊷ SHINKANSEN
㊸ OSAKA CASTLE
㊹ BUNRAKU

COLORED ILLUSTRATIONS FOR NATURALISTS

Text in Japanese, with index in Latin or English.

First Issues (Book Size 6″ × 8″)

1. BUTTERFLIES of JAPAN
2. INSECTS of JAPAN vol.1
3. INSECTS of JAPAN vol.2
4. SHELLS of JAPAN vol.1
5. FISHES of JAPAN vol.1
6. BIRDS of JAPAN
7. MAMMALS of JAPAN
8. SEA SHORE ANIMALS of JAPAN
9. GARDEN FLOWERS vol.1
10. GARDEN FLOWERS vol.2
11. ROSES and ORCHIDS
12. ALPINE FLORA of JAPAN vol.1
13. ROCKS
14. ECONOMIC MINERALS
15. HERBACEOUS PLANTS of JAPAN vol.1
16. HERBACEOUS PLANTS of JAPAN vol.2
17. HERBACEOUS PLANTS of JAPAN vol.3
18. SEAWEEDS of JAPAN
19. TREES and SHRUBS of JAPAN
20. EXOTIC AQUARIUM FISHES vol.1
21. MOTHS of JAPAN vol.1
22. MOTHS of JAPAN vol.2
23. FUNGI of JAPAN vol.1
24. PTERIDOPHYTA of JAPAN
25. SHELLS of JAPAN vol.2
26. FISHES of JAPAN vol.2
27. EXOTIC AQUARIUM FISHES vol.2
28. ALPINE FLORA of JAPAN vol.2
29. FRUITS
30. REPTILES and AMPHIBIANS of JAPAN
31. ECONOMIC MINERALS vol.2
32. FRESHWATER FISHES of JAPAN
33. GARDEN PLANTS of the WORLD vol.1
34. GARDEN PLANTS of the WORLD vol.2
35. GARDEN PLANTS of the WORLD vol.3
36. GARDEN PLANTS of the WORLD vol.4
37. GARDEN PLANTS of the WORLD vol.5
38. THE FRESHWATER PLANKTON of JAPAN
39. MEDICINAL PLANTS of JAPAN

SHELLS OF THE WESTERN PACIFIC IN COLOR

Book Size 7″×10″

⟨vol. Ⅰ⟩ by Tetsuaki Kira
(304 pages, 72 in color)
⟨vol. Ⅱ⟩ by Tadashige Habe
(304 pages, 66 in color)

FISHES OF JAPAN IN COLOR

Book Size 7″×10″

by Toshiji Kamohara
(210 pages, 64 in color)